Praise for *What We Do with God*

"These poems are sharp and precise, and the engine of them, I believe, is generosity—the generosity of Daniella Toosie-Watson, who sees the poem inside of the poem, sees the poem within the smallest insect, the smallest moment on the television screen that you do not see. What a gift this book is."

—Hanif Abdurraqib, author of *There's Always This Year*

"Do not mistake the whimsy and irreverence blooming through this collection as a lack of gravity—it is quite the opposite. These poems reinforce how brutally essential a playful imagination is to reckon with a deadly world where faith and grace are hard-earned. Toosie-Watson has compiled a glorious collection burning bright with a wild wit and an even more ferocious wisdom."

—Tarfia Faizullah, author of *Seam* and *Registers of Illuminated Villages*

"*What We Do with God* is a book of thresholds, with each poem mapping a divine passage in the body into language. Grounded, intimate, and embodied, these poems alchemize the mysterious tension between body and spirit—to revel in being vulnerable to become holy, to experience the tenderness of God in the mundane, to know mercy by knowing oneself. This is a luminous collection; Toosie-Watson is a transformational poet."

—Vanessa Angélica Villarreal, author of *Magical/Realism*

"The question in Daniella Toosie-Watson's poem 'The Bug' is 'Is this a leap?' Absolutely. A leap over or onto a prone body or a chasm. A leap from one country to another state of mind. A leap into iterations of circumstances, then, at last, beyond. *What We Do with God* is a daring, vulnerable, and uncanny book that dares to consider 'God' transmutable. Toosie-Watson doesn't shy away from animalia, mortality, the maternal, or God. Here, the body may change its form, and the form itself might change its mind. If there is a mind–body–spirit separation, Toosie-Watson isn't having it. God and sex are not at war but intertwined, are . . . of a piece. Expect only the utterly unexpected. Even the titles startle, as in 'The Dead Rat Will Remind You of Your Dad and You Won't Sleep for Weeks.' After reading this, I won't. Toosie-Watson writes, 'Love is not a coward,' and upon reading this astonishing first book, you will know: neither is she."

—Vievee Francis, author of *The Shared World*

What We Do with God

Poems

Daniella Toosie-Watson

Haymarket Books
Chicago, IL

© 2025 Daniella Toosie-Watson

Published in 2025 by
Haymarket Books
P.O. Box 180165
Chicago, IL 60618
773-583-7884
www.haymarketbooks.org
info@haymarketbooks.org

ISBN: 979-888890-370-4

Distributed to the trade in the US through Consortium Book Sales and Distribution (www.cbsd.com) and internationally through Ingram Publisher Services International (www.ingramcontent.com).

This book was published with the generous support of Lannan Foundation, Marguerite Casey Foundation, and Wallace Action Fund.

Special discounts are available for bulk purchases by organizations and institutions. Please email info@haymarketbooks.org for more information.

Cover design by Thomas Colligan.

Printed in the United States.

Library of Congress Cataloging-in-Publication data is available.
Library of Congress Control Number: 2025938075

10 9 8 7 6 5 4 3 2 1

For Gabby

*You shouldn't look at me like that. Like one of those
saints
on whom the birds once settled freely.*
　—Carl Phillips

It was grotesque, yes. But it indicated the desire for beauty.
　—Zora Neale Hurston

Contents

The Bug 1

I

all about bears 5

Pobre Charlie 9

Variations on a Theme by Ovid 10

Mom Belly Dances and Sees the Dead 11

In This Poem, My White, Jesus-Loving Dad with Glasses and Bad Jokes
   Is Not Dead 12

Sometimes I Dream of the Children I Don't Have and Miss Them
   in the Morning 14

On Flashbacks; or, When a Chickadee Sings *Chickadee*, She Knows
   Something Is Trying to Kill Her 19

The Man I Do Not Sleep With 23

Reading a Novel, Then, a Wasp 24

I Call on Memory 26

The Dead Rat Will Remind You of Your Dad and You Won't Sleep
   for Weeks 28

The Obsession to Be Good 29

Thank You for Touching Me 31

II

On the TV Screen of the Psychosis Center, the Receptionist Plays
  Horton Hears a Who! 35

Hallucination #1 37

Hallucination #2 38

Praying After Sex Is My Genre 39

Maybe God Can't Dance 40

Questions After Reading Kafka in Eleventh Grade 42

The Illness Laments 43

In 1995 the Italian Virgin Mary Statue Cried Blood; I'm Puerto Rican
  in Brooklyn and Can't Get Mercy 44

III

The Cliffs: A Love Poem 47

God Is *Dog* Spelled Backward 49

Santería 50

Maybe God Can't Dance #2 51

¡Wepa! 52

On Visiting Puerto Rico for the First Time 53

Nocturne on Fucking the Man You Met Yesterday 54

Postmortem Cleanup	55
Cedar Waxwing	56
Against Shame	57
On Grief	58
A Series of Small Miracles	60
On Mercy	61
Acknowledgments	63
Gratitude	64

The Bug

I couldn't let it drown. I ripped off a piece
of my sandwich bag, lifted it to safety.
Its little legs reached behind its back
to stroke its wings dry.
I, too, have stretched my legs
in strange positions. Is this a leap?
What did you expect? For me to let the bug
just be a bug. To leave it alone
when it already planned on dying.
To reach out and not imagine myself the God
I wish would lift me from the water.

I

all about bears

Any good artist knows
you don't try to draw a face,

or an eye, or a bear: just the lines
and shapes and eventually you'll have

a face, or an eye, or an artist drawing herself
into a bear's arms.

I don't like bears. I can't look
at the bear, face to rendered face.

Instead, I look at each line
that eventually forms fur

and fur, fur and lines that eventually
form two eyes, a long snout

with a nose at the tip of it.
Then, the woman. She lies

in the bear's arms. The fur
and fat are comfortable

against her small, human body.
Comforting, even to be held by a bear.

To be loved by what could easily kill you.
I think I understand.

I've brought plenty of men into my house.

*

In *all about love*, bell hooks says
there is a difference between care & affection,

and love. My affectionate men
rest on my stomach after swimming

in me. Bears can swim, you know. Climb, too.
How could you get away

once he's there in front of you? You don't.
It's in the bear's hands, now:

your life, your death, everything
you've tried to run from in the shape

of an animal large as anything
you've seen. Knowing this, still,

the artist draws herself
into the bear's arms. What does she know

that I don't? Who has loved her?

*

In the film *Midsommar*, Dani sacrifices
her boyfriend to cleanse the sins

of her commune. First, the elders
paralyze him. Then, they teach young boys

to carve out the inside of a bear
they've killed for the ceremony. The elders

are gentle, guide the young hands
holding the scalpels. When the bear

is disemboweled, they deposit Dani's lover
into its skin. Now it is like a man

possessed by a spirit, filled and only able
to move at the whim of that which fills it.

But the man is paralyzed. Finally,
they set the man-bear on fire inside

a wooden temple on a vast field.
It's a blue day. Good weather.

Someone, somewhere, is outside reading
their favorite book of poetry for ceremony.

Dani's people watch and wail, convulse
their bodies as the man burns. He's so quiet.

Only his eyes can move,
like a portrait of a woman

and a bear: their eyes watch when you walk
to the other side of the room.

Any well-rendered portrait will follow you.
The artist smiles. Dani's people are clean.

The whole time I know the inside of the bear
is wet, cushioned with flesh like my vagina.

Yes, the fire. I know the inside of the bear
is touching his skin. He's wearing

the thing I fear most like a new dress,
like the one on the artist who draws herself

in the bear's arms. I have this recurring dream
of bears breaking into my house. In the first few,

I could keep the door shut
against the muscle of the bear. Lately,

instead of holding the door, I find an escape route.
Apostle Paul says we must die for Christ

to live in us. I love Jesus, as my lovers do. Let us
die together then.

Is it worth it? To be killed
by what could easily love you.

Please don't kill me, lover. I won't sacrifice
you. Just let the bear inside.

Pobre Charlie

Charlie the Llama was attacked
by our rottweiler while Mom wasn't watching.
Back in the day, in the Bronx, Mom left Dad
in the back with the dog pack
while she got the lemonade.
The dogs ripped the weakest
in the pack limb from limb. Mom says
animals are a safe intimacy,
but that's because she's the alpha.
The head of the pack. Top dog.
Her chihuahua, Peanut, bit and tugged
at the back of my pajamas. Mom teased me
for how little the pack respects me.

Charlie recovered from the dog attack.
When he was finally able to walk again,
Mom brought him inside to tend
to his wounds and he slipped,
hit his head on the radiator.
He died right there.
It's never what you think is going to kill you.
Except it is. When I die, I'll do it myself.
When I was twenty-five, before ever having had sex,
I bought a vibrator and penetrated myself first
so no one could say they took anything from me.

Variations on a Theme by Ovid

Like any other reasonable children who want to play
with their small goat but don't know how to explain
their games because they don't know enough goat words,
my brother and I strap on skateboard helmets
and take turns headbutting with Roger.
What else did she expect us to do?
I'm not saying my mom's the devil when she's angry,
but I've seen a goat: I gallop towards Roger with unfamiliar legs,
losing human form with each strike. I know horns
when I see them. No one will recognize me.
I'll look nothing like my mom.

Mom Belly Dances and Sees the Dead

Sitting at my kitchen table,
I watch the wind
remember Mom's coin scarf.

The wind is pleased
by the shimmying
leaves, exaggerated

by shadow and almost-gone
light. I know envy
when I see it. But my mom

wants to die. *You're old enough
to live without me*, she says,
and I am seven again,

and she is a purple
and blue whirlwind
of bedlah, her feet, rapturing

through the grass, her hands,
flitting the air as if brushing
back death. I want to tell her

there are things to live for,
but she sees
spirits of the dead

and envies them.
Don't look at me like that.
You who live

without magic and miracle.
I let out a deep breath.
The leaves rustle again.

In This Poem, My White, Jesus-Loving Dad with Glasses and Bad Jokes Is Not Dead

I didn't say God isn't real.
It's that I can't get a read on him.
I'm not a seer,
but I do have dreams.
They are not like the hallucinations,
though those are real, too. I mean
I have a lineage. God gave Mami
a tiny car made of light when she was a child.
Little Mami picked up the little car,
flew it through the air. Mami tells me
this story when I tell her the psychiatrist
says I have psychosis. Mami rebuts
that I am the blessed of the Lord.
I don't think my Dead Dad—
when he was my Alive Dad—knew
that me and Mami are the blessed of the Lord.
Dead Dad knows now.
One Sunday at church,
I asked the pastor, *if Jesus is God,
then how come the men could pull
at His beard and hit Him*,
as I gestured at my own nine-year-old,
imaginary beard and swung at the air.
After service, Alive Dad told me
I had asked a good question.
Alive Dad led children's Bible study
before Sunday service. There was one kid
we called the bad-joke kid.
The answer to his joke
was always, *a giant donut*,
and he'd let out a laugh as wide
as the chasm between heaven and hell.
He wore glasses, if I remember correctly.
He was white. Alive Dad also wore
glasses and was white. Maybe I'm conflating the two.
But the child was real. I don't know

if I misremember often. Make no mistake,
my dad is alive in this poem.
His glasses are on, his skin is white,
and his jokes are bad. He likes
cozy snacks and plays videos games
with us on the weekends and loves Jesus.
Jesus is his favorite.
I ask him if he loves God or me more,
and he says he has to love God more.
In this poem, he loves me more.
The pastor never did answer my question,
but I remember feeling what Mom feels
when she uses her psychic powers
to gauge if someone is lying. Empty,
like something is missing. I don't know if my white,
glasses-adorned, Jesus-loving,
Alive Dad who told bad jokes knew
that Mom is psychic. Mom says
I have the same gifts as her and my great-grandma.
It's our Puerto Rican, matriarchal lineage.
Alive Dad would be pissed if he knew
Mom saw his Dead Dad ghost
in our living room. Joke's on you,
white, glasses-wearing, Jesus-loving Alive Dad.
Dead Dad knows how to take a joke.
Knock, knock.
It's Jesus, back from hell.

Sometimes I Dream of the Children I Don't Have and Miss Them in the Morning

It was the slippery shoes and a too-long dress.
My mother told me not to run; I told her,

what do you know of past lives? The man
who bandaged my arm wore headphones,

nodded his head, rocked his body, and popped
gum that cracked like knuckle cartilage

before you find yourself on the floor
with a radiating heat on the left side of your face.

It feels how a siren sounds.
Never talk about someone's mother.

                       The man laid white strips
across my arm like a gentle abuela lays
raw chicken cutlets in the oil. You wouldn't know

but for my telling you that I remember him.
But now that I'm in love, I have chosen
I will forget him. I'll forget every *you,*

now that I'm in love. No, I wasn't dragged
by the collar. I was surrounded
by plush green, green, green. After the dirt
was wet, I jabbed my fingers into the soft
mound, soft as my belly.

                     I had to be gentle
when the soil was dry. I made my hand
into a ladle and dipped into the hardened,
small earth of the pot and gently

scraped, gently as my gynecologist
said it would be but wasn't. *Just a small pinch.*
I still get pain flashbacks.

After pressing my finger around the surface
like the doctor presses my belly to feel
for the pain, I found the soft

spot and my finger turned into a pelican
diving for fish in water, cradled the dirt
in my palm like a newborn.

      Sometimes I dream
      of the children
      I don't have and miss them

      in the morning.
I close my eyes and listen
to the *glug, glug* of liquid
release from the bottle's nipple
into the mouth

of the ink cartridges until they are full
of color—yellow, maroon, cyan.
Night sweats out of my porous face.

Every now and then I need a Xanax.
There are night-marks on my bedsheets.
I'll have to wash them in the morning.
Oh God! There is so much to do.

My brain is sour-armpit musk masked
with peony. The sun is a cigarette
in the morning's mouth; the morning
Gene Kelly'd light into my face

but God's voice was not there. I am grease-
slick roots and half-ponytail amalgamation

of red-dyed hair. I know just how I'll do it:
I'll move myself around my bed

to make sure the sheet's tension is even
on each side. The psalmist says,
Joy comes in the morning. In the mornings,
parents walk their children to school.

Scooter wheels turn on their axles.
So many cars scattering
here and there like worker ants.
God's voice wasn't in the earthquake

or the mighty wind. It was a whisper
that brought the prophet
to the cave's mouth. I open the window's
mouth and shout, *Shut the fuck up—God*

is talking. I wipe night
from my forehead, dry my palm
on my bedsheet. The morning leaned
against the wall of my room, kissed me

yellow. Here's a trick: put your thumb
in your mouth and pull it out quick,
like a lollipop—your lipstick
won't get on your teeth. I wish

I had a thumb to suck on.
I move my tongue between my lip
and teeth like a credit card. I crawl

under my covers, still night-wet.
The morning is loud. I rub my thumb
on my teeth until they squeak again.
I could use a Xanax.
                      You understand,
                      don't you?

What We Do with God

Trace your thumb
along my mouth, baby. I'll shower for you.

                I have a terrible memory
of who I was before I was born.
It's said the spirit chooses
the family they are born into.
Suckling on my mother's nipple,
in the language I thought in,
I looked up at her sweating,
smiling face and said, *I chose you; I chose you.*

                I don't know if I'll remember
my death in my new, sky-filled life.
I imagine it will be all I have ever known:
being free. Before my death, my mother took me
to the mountain to swim in its lake.
The water was leech-infested. She told me
to get out of the water; I told her,
you're not my only mother.

It's easy to tell the truth when you've been slighted.
Love makes you lie.

Love has just arrived
from the protest in a raincoat
as yellow as a cliché is a cliché.
Love will never be yellow
unless the whites of your lover's eyes
have been whisked with malady's yolk.
Unless it is the sun weeping over
the world. The world, a war—
this is not a metaphor, and
love is not a coward. Love is not a coward.

                This fascist regime
will fall and break every bone
in its body, in its goddamned body.
What will I tell my mother

when the guns crack like the body
of man when it fell from grace
to this hell-paved earth
and I'm bloodied from war
and I wake the next morning,
looking up at another woman's face,
babbling, again: *I chose you; I chose you.*
My new-mother doesn't watch as I swim.
Save me, old-mother. The water
is cold. My hands, blue.
It's time to come inside.

On Flashbacks; or, When a Chickadee Sings *Chickadee,* She Knows Something Is Trying to Kill Her

I floundered in a riptide.
Before a group of women
pulled me out of the water

I looked up at the sky,
witnessed sorbet clouds spill
across the expanse like God

were a messy child
eating ice cream.
I was about to master

something beautiful.
All the waves
applauded the final act.

The tide gripped me
like a reluctant womb.
Do you remember your birth?

Who does, am I right? My name rang
across the sound and I answered the call,
closed my eyes. The women peeled my body

from the water like you peeled
a sleeping man's arm
from across your chest at 2 a.m.,

the man you just met who told you during sex
that he loves you. It's always like that,
isn't it? One moment you're swimming, gasping

in pleasure, the next, you're sitting at your kitchen table
hoping not to die. It took one woman
per limb to pull me out.

I'm nothing
remarkable,
but I'm alive.

At my kitchen table, where I sat to chop
the cilantro for the sofrito the day prior
because standing is hard these days,

I hear my neighbor's voice
emerge from the window below
and into my kitchen.

She always sings
Amy Winehouse's "Valerie."
Sometimes I record

myself singing. I never sound how I think.
I swore my voice was Amy Winehouse's
when I started practicing "Valerie,"

until I finally listened
to the recording and I deleted it
faster than you can say:

I wish I told my neighbor that I love her
singing, but there is a man in my bed
who told me tonight he loves me

and I don't want to die.
What else to make of someone
who loves so quickly but a murderer?

Would you like to have sex,
together? I ask my neighbor one night
on the apartment complex's front lawn.

What We Do with God

It never sounds how you plan it.
She declines, and we lay our bodies
back into the ocean

of grass, staring up at the sorbet sky. God
has so many treats his teeth
are rotten. Like a consciousness

peeling back its human form,
I peel my forehead off
of my arm. I'm in a daze

from my neighbor's gular fluttering.
Why don't you come on over?
Look at me, humming along

as if I, too, had chickadees emerging from my throat.
Look at me, hanging over my kitchen table until
the morning hours that mother me.

The sorbet light covers my skin
like a bandage. My puppy licks
my ankles to wake me

or love me. I am nothing
remarkable, but I'm alive.
Look at me, how disheveled: everyone

must think I've just had sex or something.
I did just have sex or something.
Exhilarating, to be the hinge

upon which a life changes
from *funny to see you here*
to *I remember the water.*

Listen to "Valerie" emerge, clothed in nothing
but my neighbor's voice.
I wish my name were Valerie.

I'd descend the apartment stairs,
knock on the door,
answer the call.

The Man I Do Not Sleep With

Harlem, NY

In Morningside Park we lie in the grass, high,
the sky the kind of blue you see
when you're high like we are: brighter,
more welcoming, more ready to take you in,
not like a swallowing, no, but like sex, as in, if I
were to have it with you, if I could have it at all.
Now here comes the cliché:
two butterflies above your chest,
hovering there, and it's true.
This grass could be a bed if it were not grass.
I remember my body, under my clothes
is skin, and I might as well not
be wearing clothes at all.

I assume the turtles are still piling on one another
scrambling for food on the water.
The crane, too, must still be there.
Unless it's only in my mind that it stayed
where I last saw it. I hope the crane has gone
wherever it would like to be.
And I wish I could be more animal.
Not thinking about what it might cost me.

Reading a Novel, Then, a Wasp

for Tyriek White

Tenderness sears
the cityscape
of ghost bodies
ascending into a peach-
skin-soft sky.
Buildings sigh,
silo the street
a valley. Apartments
with more eyes
than a host of seraphim
guard the children—
                then, a wasp.

The novel's images
swell like a bubble
pregnant with breath—bigger,
bigger—until the final
exhale, its release. The wasp
        bucks.   Then,
        crawls
like a baby into the grass.
Who can stand
to stay?

            Wings coo.
The grass's tiny
green limbs want
towards its sky-mother.
The wasp turns into itself
(further, further)
as if to pierce itself like a god-
worshipping pagan
mourns their dead.
A fetus curled
and ready to be born—

the fucking thing that stung me
to its end—
joins the fiction
of ghosts. I turn the page.
The wasp ascends
against the backdrop
of a star-dewed sky.

I Call on Memory

Just when I almost have you
in my mind's eye, you are a crane in the water
at the park behind my grandmother's apartment

where I was going to tell you, *I love you*,
in my new blue dress I bought because I thought
you'd like it. Once—that good night—you touched me

with your nervous mouth, a fish's lips against my skin;
my skin is water, and you, at the surface, are at the precipice
of another kind of air-filled life. We are coy, curved

into each other like a ballerina's feet en pointe.
Our fish bodies writhe, each slit of our ribs ripple
in the wake of our rapid breath. My mouth widens

like a siren's wail. My heart of sinew, sinew:
rippling, rippling. You slippery, finned thing:
you're a feathered, fantastic ice-dancer again,

scaling the pond's surface with your delicate claws.
I call on memory. When the night came to tell you,
I love you, in my blue dress: you raped me.

I almost have it. But then the narrative: I didn't know
I was raped, until the nurse told me, *stealthing is rape*.
And then, I fucked eight different people in a week.

And then, you are a man.
Where did your scales go?
Those little sequins that splayed

sunbeams like a filet blade?
Look: I tossed them to the pond like pennies.
I wished the water red as my polish-slick,

acrylic nail that circled my fin-thin clit, that good night.
You wear the water like a new skin, or a pretty dress.

The Dead Rat Will Remind You of Your Dad and You Won't Sleep for Weeks

Did you know a dead rat's eyes wither like grapes
within hours of dying? I know because I held
my dear rat for eight hours before I let her go.

Aesthetically speaking, a dead animal looks better
than a dead person because fur covers the paling skin.
Have you ever been with a dead animal long enough
to feel it harden against you, like a cock on your back?
She died on my chest. Her body jerked. Violently,
eight times, before going still.

What We Do with God

The Obsession to Be Good

After a while you can't smell the animals
on your clothes, not because the smell went away.
Unless there is another explanation,
you adjust to the scent and you don't notice
the monitor lizard's piss until someone
asks about the smell and you will realize
that you shouldn't have left class to use the bathroom
because then your classmates will know
the smell is gone in your absence and it was you.
I look terrible, my English teacher tells me.
I wear a photo of my dad on my shirt under my dog-haired
sweatshirt to keep him close. I don't want to talk about it.

Now, I'm older and I smell good.
I'm coming for your man.
No, I don't want him, but you should both know
I'd be the better choice.
Look what it's done to me. Look what I've done.
I don't leave the house without perfume.
The animals are coming back to bite me on the ass,
as it were. I ask with a floral mouth if he likes the smell
of my perfume, he says he doesn't like the scent of chemicals.
I'm a monitor lizard again, living
in the bathroom and the child dropped her pants in my piss
but wore them anyway. I'm a pig living in the kitchen
and rubbed my snout on her leg saying,
please, love me before you go.
I'm a dog's wet mouth. I wag my fast tail at everyone's man.
If he's going to be my boyfriend, he needs to love
Jesus. So, I take him to Wednesday night Bible study.
I'm waiting for marriage. I'm waiting for God.
I'm waiting to write the wreck,[*] as it were, not about the wreck.
How to render it, you know what I mean:
the unspeakable thing. Not make meaning of it,
the meaning of it is the life I'm living. Animals,

---

[*] Adrienne Rich, "Diving into the Wreck," in *Diving into the Wreck: Poems 1971–1972* (New York: Norton, 1973).

like God,
are a safe intimacy. Mom says, so, she ushers them in:
rottweilers, snakes, hissing
cockroaches. Call the deacon. My body,
my God. Look at what my God has rendered. All this skin
and skin. All this ass. I'm all the things I will never be.
It's called adjacency. It's called spite. It's called obsession.
Even the water smells
like a dog's wet mouth. I bathe in it getting ready for school.
I douse myself in perfume hoping
your boyfriend will like it. Hoping you'll be my friend.
I'm the pretty friend. Pretty, pretty. Pretty girl
has her dad's eyes. I'll never see him again.
And that's fine. It's all fine. I go to school. I do the job.
At church with your boyfriend, the prophet says,
you have daddy issues. You don't know me, bitch.
"Thus sayeth the Lord" will have you in hot water with God.
Who did I prophesy to? What did I do wrong?
I didn't want the assault. I didn't want it, I didn't want it.
Please, take my memory away.

Thank You for Touching Me

I tell the crowd at your reading that I'm
funny then read a poem about death

and masturbation. Little deaths, little
deaths. I'm on a sex break. I hate being touched.

There are fingers stuck to my clothes. Fingers
appear like sequins. I shouldn't have washed

that dress. Fingers appear like spirits when
your god isn't listening. Sequins are

everywhere I go. In his shoe, one went
home with my favorite lover.

In the cab to my apartment after
your reading, you picked a sequin off my

shoulder and placed it on my cheek. Placed it
where Marilyn Monroe's beauty mark is,

if my face was Marylin Monroe's.
My pussy is fantastic. God is a god

of little deaths. I die all the time.

The preacher said, *God is closer to us
than we are to ourselves*, then fingered me

while I was on my period. Blood was
on his hands. I put my fingers in your

hair. We made nervous love until we died.
In the morning we rushed to the ER.

The doctor blew a kiss to God when I
survived sepsis and it landed on His

cheek, where Marilyn Monroe's beauty mark
is, if His face was Marilyn Monroe's.

God replies to prayers like a drunk man
stumbling out of a cab at 2 a.m.

God is a god of little deaths. I die all the time.
Except when God won't let me. Isn't it funny?

II

On the TV Screen of the Psychosis Center, the Receptionist Plays *Horton Hears a Who!*

A person is a person, no matter how small.
       —Dr. Seuss, *Horton Hears a Who!*

The elephant in the room
hears voices and my psychiatrist wants
to be my lover. My psychiatrist—whose wife
is jealous of me for being sixteen and pretty—

says that if you could articulate
God, you could hold him
in the palm of your hand.
When my psychiatrist asks me if I can hear God

the elephant enters
the evaluation room
and says, *A voice is a voice,
no matter how small.*

        Not now, Horton, I say,
don't you know, it's not good to be alive?
My psychiatrist's wife calls to ask who
he is in session with. He says he's with me.

Are you serious? she yells, and he winks,
leaves the room. The elephant takes
the pink clover from behind his ear
and tucks it behind mine. Now I'm thirty-two

and the husband and wife are still arguing
in the other room and the elephant still
sits next to me. How did the wife know me?
How could I know God? If I knew God,

I could hold him
in the palm of my hand.
The elephant in the room tells me,

a god is a god, no matter how small.

                Not now, Horton, I say.
I say, *don't you know my psychiatrist
wanted to be my lover?* My mother says
I'm selfish, but there's nothing

I know better than my way around a dick
and doesn't that make me unselfish?
I'm a gracious lover. Reader,
can we be lovers? Can you hold me

like a dog holds little dogs in their mouths?
Yes, let's be lovers, and romanticize
the music from the speaker. Let's kiss
in the sudden, embellished park:

the heat's skin pressing down on us—
harder. Harder, now. Just as I lean in
to kiss you, I want to die. Here comes Horton, saying,
a life is a life, no matter how small.

                Not now, Horton.
It's not good to be alive, but it's good
to be alive and not want to die.
My new psychiatrist prescribes Abilify

and Horton takes the pink clover from behind my ear,
before he leaves: pets my hair.

Hallucination #1

I am six, dreaming. A library window
frames the street, the beige

Cadillac holds
the man whose eyes

are disappearing. He is screaming.
A clown is crossing the cross

walk away from him. The clown's head hovers
over the stacks now. I leave the window to hide.

I am 29. The otherwise night is now lit.
I wake to a clown floating,

florescent, in the center
of the room laughing, digging

a hole. I close my eyes,
open—the clown is laughing, digging

a hole. I close
my eyes—

digging a hole, laughing still:
I remember the man with fading eyes.

I open my mine—the clown,
plays the shovel as a gun,

shooting into a distance
I can't see.

Hallucination #2

Glowstick butterfly—child-grabbed,
cracked in half
light. You flame-sputter fly
toward my face, then, you are suspended
next to my head and spinning
into an amalgamation
of black antenna, little legs
      tighter, tighter,
until you disappear.
      Your end?
The reason you are here—a reason
I don't know—pinches you
between two fingers and threads
you back into my room. You spindle, spindle—
child at the dizzied moment
before her fall—back into florescent
orange wings, flying away from me, then, gone again

Praying After Sex Is My Genre

On the night we met, my new lover and I fucked,
then prayed to thank God for great sex.
In the morning, he was a vision.
I was handed a cup of ginger tea.
I dreamt you were here, and here
you are. The water boiled. Sleep
took me.

Clouds pinked my lover's face.
We prayed naked. God watched. *Be careful, it's hot*,
but that's not why I don't take the cup—I was tired.
You're a vision, I smile and touch his face.
Tiny lights and vines braid around the black pipes above
his bed. My eyes blur. His perfect mouth
kisses me. He asks me
to edit his poetry manuscript. I put on my editor's hat.
Fucking is my wheelhouse. A past lover played gospel
instead of something sexy
to prevent my panic attacks.

                After I dream,
I wake up alone. Except when I hallucinate.
One night in August, I woke up next to my childhood
best friend. She was smiling into a distance. It's March now.
His writing is expository in ways that don't serve the poem.
I take the ginger tea. He kisses my forehead.
I blow the cloud, but the tea is still breathing.
He asks me to leave. My first hallucination this year
was a flower—opening, and opening, and opening

Maybe God Can't Dance

1.
Always, on a Saturday night, the floor is hard
beneath me, the men are at my mercy,
and the music sweating and smiling and here.
In the discoteca I spin, the wood rises and ripples
at my feet, amén.
In the discoteca you
should be ashamed should be ashamed should be ashamed
for calling unclean what God has called clean. Look at me: I am sexy.
Jesus raises his glass. The water rises at my feet and then, a cloud
of prophecy, hovering.
In the doorway,
the doctor appears,
calls me in to test for psychosis.

2.
Do
you even get   horny Pastor's
wife says   you're tainted
for wanting   sex Says
jezebel Says *those cult- ural danc es aren't*
of God. Says *you need a demon cast out.*
The doctor says
Who do you hear?
Do you believe
you have superpowers? God—
do you hear him? Does God give you
superpowers? Who do you hear?
What do the voices tell you?
Racist? If it's a part of your culture,
then it's not psychosis.
And then God struck them both dead.

3.
The therapist sent me to the psychosis
center. I told her I hear God.
My pills keep vigil from my bookshelf.

There are so many. I would take them
all at once, but my niece is six
and I braid her hair best. I am sick. Or
I'm blessed.

4.
The Spirit and I copa
to the discoteca, they
tell me to prophesy to
raise the doctor and pastor.
I shimmy my chest and the
women's bones become claves and come
together but there is no
flesh so then I make my leg
latigazo and behold,
flesh. The bodies have no breath,
so the Spirit says *¡otra
vez!* so I spin and water
rises through the floorboards, wakes
the women but they have no
rhythm. So, the Spirit tells
me to cry *¡WEPA!* and the
women wail *¡WEPA!* press to-
gether, skin to skin, hip to
hip, wining their waists and step-
ping in count, light ushering
in from behind them, like a
sedative pushing through the
barrel of a syringe.

Questions After Reading Kafka in Eleventh Grade

If a woman can turn to salt, and Jesus can transfigure,
or rise from the dead, a man definitely can become
a giant bug. If my mom could see the ghost of an old man
in her apartment, finding out later that an old man had,
in fact, died and been left there a week before
the neighbors smelled the stench, then, of course,
I can have visions and hear voices, too. Mom calls it
lineage. My psychiatrist prescribes medication. I still hear God.
Kafka and Dad both died on June 3. It makes sense,
the reaction of Kafka's vulture: fly up in the air, dive
right down into the man's throat, even if it means
drowning in his blood. The vulture was going to die
either way. Why not choose? Try to make death
mean something. If my mom saw an old man
in her apartment, then I believe she saw my dead dad. Dad didn't believe
in ghosts. Why become one? It's not useful to stick
to a story. Living was a story. When you were cremated
and Mom said we'd each get a part of you,
my ten-year-old brain didn't know what cremation meant.
I wanted your hand with the ring still on it—
you never hit me with it. I'd preserve it in a jar
on the shelf above my bed.
Keep my mother's hands. Both of them.

The Illness Laments

It's always scary
when she takes the medicine.

One moment, I am a free body
of spattering light.

Then, I am shifting shadow stitched
and tugging against the bright seams,

loosening but not loosed.
Now, she's taut, slick against me.

In 1995 the Italian Virgin Mary Statue Cried Blood; I'm Puerto Rican in Brooklyn and Can't Get Mercy

—you must hate me now, too. In the waiting room,
the blood Virgin-Mary'd from my eyes. Witnesses say
deer trotted across the field of my face to lap up
the miracle. The now-carnivorous deer leapt
like Elizabeth's baby, red-mouthed, heads all wagging,
limp-necked flags in a cool wind. The doctor won't see me.
I don't want her to die, but she hates me, now that I've arrived
late, and what am I to do with the weight of all this.
The red mascara I painted on this morning to look prettier
than you stripes my face a flag. Everything is cinema.
Trees talk to each other, did you know? All chisme,
and you aren't in on the joke. Plants don't bleed like us
hearted ones. Veins fern just under my skin,
saying *yes, just like that. And there. There, too.*
Yet the phlebotomists can never find the right spot.
All the women hate me and all the women look
like family. God straddled the desk between me
and the receptionist like a girl at recess, legs
on either side of the bench saying, *don't worry
about her, bitch, your butt is getting bigger—
it's the men you've been eating,* and just as the trees
laugh because they get the joke, the boys call us
over from the window of their tech class and say, *not you,
just the pretty one.* The waiting room watched me cry.
God wept with me and our eyes bled together.
Don't worry, Lord—everyone praises your blood.
Mine is just makeup.

III

The Cliffs: A Love Poem

The ledge was worse
than the jump.

My body was an ancient,
crystallized bug:

suspended, the rush
of water suddenly

muted when I left
this life for the breathless

kind. It was early morning.
Prayers swarmed God

like a cloud
of gnats. Overworked,

eyes low like mine
when I was injected

with morphine, He said,
It's always like this,

wiped the table down.
The morphine warmed my body

like it was adjusting to water,
or new love. I didn't know

what sepsis meant, so death
didn't occur to me—

until I asked the doctor
for a therapist

but he sent a chaplain.
It's like that, isn't it?

No one wants to be the one to say it:
Death. Death, death, death.

Anyway, the ledge
was a rock, not the cliff

other people dove from.
It might as well have been—

my fear was proportional to the height of it.

I passed
through the water

like a kidney stone.
What I'm saying is,

this is how
I love you:

it took everything from me
to throw myself in.

God Is *Dog* Spelled Backward

Listen, this god is huge. Mom always says not to run
from gods, but when our new Doberman, Optimus,
leaps up on her hind legs and lunges for her throat,
I'm Jonah running from his calling. My mother, leaning against
the kitchen counter in her white and blue night gown,
hair a cloud of curling, black smoke, eyes low like she'd
just been drunk with the Holy Spirit. Not as in out drinking
with the Holy Spirit. Him lamenting that he'd created man;
her lamenting about her own children and how much they cost.
As in, he entered her body. But not as in sex, or possession
(though maybe sex and possession?). Optimus jumps on Mom
and she says Optimus isn't a bad god, just doing what gods do: wanting
to be head of the pack, top god. Her boyfriend runs
in from the living room and puts Optimus in a chokehold,
wrestles her to the floor, wraps his legs around the writhing
god until she submits. Mom chastises me for running.
Said she thought she trained me better. What prophet
sang "Holy, Holy" without first grieving her life. Maybe Mary.
Maybe my mother. When Optimus dies in her old age, my mother
cries for weeks. I was afraid of that bitch until her last
breath. O, dog, my mother laments. Huge dog. Dog of wonders.
Dog, I've seen what you've done for others. Dog of Mary. My god,
my god—my god is gone.

Santería

Someone in my family must have known it.
Perhaps it was my mother. Late
morning. Water rose as she sang. A fit
of fish gasped, so she sang louder. As fate
would have it, the water rose at such rates
that waves washed across the room. Maybe,
though, it was known before her. The gods ate
my grandma's Ebó and were filled. Or she
might not know, and I am a special saint.

Maybe God Can't Dance #2

We dance　　　　　　　　　　　like incense smoke
　　　　　　　　　　　　　　　　from the worshippers' throats

The spirits and I　　　　　　　　dance in my room
nunca en linea　　　　　　　　　lest you want
to be less free.

Rebuke anyone who　　says　　a little cumbia in your salsa
isn't orderly.

How can you follow　　　　　　God
a bad salsero who　　　　　　　won't know the count.

Forgets　　　　　　　　　　　devotion—
I am　　　　　　　　　　　　　the Orishas' twirl

the galaxy　　　　　　　　　　the discoteca

across the room　　　　　　　　while God cries
in the corner free　　　　　　　　styling alone.

¡Wepa!

My blood is so hot and wet right now.
I know they want it.
 —Morgan Parker

Why did I kill them?   At the party I yelled *¡wepa!* & just before I closed my mouth a white woman grabbed my tongue & cut it out. The horn wailed; kept vigil for eight counts. She tied my tongue to a string & hung it around her neck. I lunged for her neck but just then a white man grabbed my hand for a dance. He was an aggressive lead, but I couldn't say no—my cheeks were filling with blood. He spun me.

Each spin was more aggressive than the last & reminded of what I'd lost. Behind him at the door I saw the white woman & I tried to spot my tongue, but she'd acquired new tongues, so I couldn't tell mine from the others. I was dizzy, but I couldn't spill the blood, so I spotted using the bundle of tongues around her neck until I spun again & she was gone. I fell. The white man did not try to catch me & was angry that I'd ruined his dance.

I left the party to find someplace to spill all the blood until, gracias a Dios, I spotted a Latino. I wanted to ask him for direction, but remember, my mouth was filling with blood, but I was sure, yes, I was sure he'd seen women in my condition & any moment now he'd recognize me. You must be Puerto Rican, he said & I wanted to cry *¡Wepa, hermano, wepa! Ayudame, por favor.* I knew it, he said, your hips & ass gave it away, & he grabbed me & forced his mouth on mine.

He should've known & I didn't wish to save him, so I opened my mouth & he drowned.

On Visiting Puerto Rico for the First Time

after Yusef Komunyakaa

Damn coquí.
Your high-pitched bleating
for a lover. My mother
said I would not see you,
only hear your voices
that now overwhelm
this balcony and pour
into the room.
Damn the coconuts
and the breeze
that moves them.
The palm trees sway,
cast a spell—a couple clangs
against one another,
laughs, stumbles up the street
where my grandmother was raised.
Perhaps they don't know
they are dying,
or perhaps they laugh
because they do.
Tonight, I'm in Puerto Rico
while my mother is dying
and my father is dead, and I don't know where
I stand in this inheritance.
        Damn the coquí.
I could step
on you if I wanted.
My mother said I would not see you,
but now, here you've arrived, coquí.
Small and grey at my feet.
Each toe, a prong,
setting the small jewel
of your body. You've been listening:
you hop off the balcony
before I can move my foot

Nocturne on Fucking the Man You Met Yesterday

It's a human need to give shapelessness a form.
    —Carl Phillips

The outside lamp's golden gaze melds the leaves
and both your bodies into a single
shadow. You trace his form, he pushes his
tongue into the inner crease of your thigh.
The fickle figure of leaf and limb shifts
as shafts of light trip, splay shadows over
and into its singular self. You know
the distance from the door to bed, each edge
of the desk and dresser. But you stay. See
your shadows move? Gilded, black waves? *Fuck me
like you love me*, he says. Love is good, then
unspeakable. Knowing this, still, you kiss
his shoulder, spread yourself—light dispersed
over the top of the water.

Postmortem Cleanup

He says, *they are dead but they are people*,

and gently peels off each bandage. After

his shift, I raise my ass like the undead.

The nurse swings his head back, howls like the rush

of a soul leaving a body. He lifts

his hand to spank me, I think of the dead.

He must have been quiet when he slid his

hand under the back of their legs, cradled

them in the bends of his elbows, carried

them to new, clean beds. Laid them down. Their skin

freshly naked of bandages, raw as

my ass is when he brings his hand—sheathed in

light like a plastic glove—down against me.

If they weren't dead, they could feel what he did.

Cedar Waxwing

after Ross Gay

I'm sitting on the front stoop of my apartment when a flock
of birds interrupts my sadness and guzzles up the berries
on the tree next to me. My neighbor walks by and I show
her the birds and she throws her arms in the air
as if she has just won or her team scored the goal or made
the shot at the buzzer and exclaims, I KNOW THOSE BIRDS,
and I ask, then please, tell me, and she tells me: cedar waxwing.
A group of which is called an "earful" or "museum," ironic
because you must be thinking, by now, what an earful
to be hearing all about these birds but at least I'm not telling you
why I was sitting on the stoop and why I didn't want to go back
into my apartment that has become a museum of my sadness
and it doesn't take much to assume why a flock of these birds
would be called an "earful" with their high-pitched trill
but in all my searching I can't find or figure out why "museum."
But did you know that cedar waxwings can get drunk from berries
that have begun to ferment and then smash themselves into windows?
Perhaps all birds are clumsily cutting through the air on a bar crawl
from tree to fermented berry tree then smashing into the glass
and one by one swirling to the ground but imagine the force
of an entire flock breaking through the window and it's a drunken
party of birds in my living room and they find me,
too, drunk on the floor, and they swoop me up in their social
whirl and their trill is now the song that we dance to and no one
can tell us that it is not a song and this time I don't take
the broken glass and I don't cut myself with it and I don't
wake up in the morning regretting the pour and the cut
and the inevitable scar and I go outside and sit on the stoop
and say thank you to the birds for being there.

Against Shame

In the back seat of his car
barely large enough to contain our writhing
bodies, the heavy fat of the moon, rippling;
and of course, his howl—*oh*
                          my god—the arch of my back: his hand
down my spine is a patient stream.

Hours to go before we sleep, I
already know, for the first time:
I won't pray for forgiveness.

On Grief

Mount Vernon, NY, summer of 2002

The pavement rivers from North Columbus Avenue
splits off into the Davis's and my grandmother's
shared driveway, streams down-

hill, opens at the mouth, and empties
into the Davis's backyard. My grandmother's backyard:
all loose rock and dirt. I swim

through our neighbors to look for my dad.
On days like today, music flows back up
into the street like a gushing fire

hydrant; the pavement ripples from basketballs pulsing
like atoms in boiling water;
the girls my age turn ropes, chanting,

feet splashing up from the floor; the adults cluster together
in white plastic chairs, gather around the grill,
laughter eddying through the rocks in their throats.

But I want to hang out with my dad. Go to the schoolyard
across the street where the giant tree in the back is our own kingdom,
where my dad and I hunt for cicada shells

and make homes for them that are always destroyed by
the next day but we rebuild them each time anyway.
I look up and see my dad laughing with my grandma on the porch

where a soft, miniature soccer ball, tied to a thin rope, hangs
next to them, the one that no matter how hard
we've punched it, has never let loose—a merciless

pendulum. *The fish is ready.* My paddling feet kick up the dust,
fragmenting the sunlight, what I now imagine my dad's
ashes would look like, floating softly toward the water

where he wanted them released that next summer,
if only I could get my damned hands
to pick him up from the shelf and let him go.

A Series of Small Miracles

after Ross Gay, after Gwendolyn Brooks

This morning
I stepped outside & the chill
kissed my forehead but only after I gave permission
& afterward I was still okay with the touch
& when I returned to my apartment,
I was okay with the leaving. But we aren't there yet.
My neighbor walked by with their dog,
stopped to let me pet her & thanked me
for doing so. & listen, now I will tell you:
today, my room is warm.
I sit on my bed. I lift my shorts.
I notice the crease between
my thigh & lower belly,
trace my finger between that small valley
& I say *it is good*. I notice my thigh, its generosity,
squeeze the fat of it. Slap it one time for good measure.
Listen: in this poem, there are no men.
I give to myself & give again.
I cup my small breast
& I'm thankful—there is no one here
to tell her that she does not have enough to give.
I play a record & my mind is clear to hear it.
Today, I lie in bed all afternoon
& it is my choice.
I breathe in & the breathing is simple. I breathe out—
a mango grove fills my room. I crawl into a cradle of branches.
I rest my head on a bunch of mangos. Yesterday, I heard
someone call out *Sorrow* & I did not turn my head.

On Mercy

No, I didn't
delight in the fruit
flies' deaths,
though anyone who
heard me scoff
would have thought
I did. One version
of myself would have
let them overrun
the kitchen. I've learned
to harden
my heart.
If I'd have let
the fruit flies live,
I'd have named
each one.
Consider how small
each of their hearts,
how much tiny
blood, the little
distances the blood
travels in those small
bodies. God of tiny
nuisances—
who counts each hair
on my head—
I am god
of them now. Stuck
to the strip,
I know some of them
are still alive.

Acknowledgments

Thank you to the journals who have published work from this collection, sometimes in an earlier form:

Oxford Poetry (Summer/Spring 2025): "In 1995 the Italian Virgin Mary Statue Cried Blood; I'm Puerto Rican in Brooklyn and Can't Get Mercy"

Michigan Quarterly Review Mixtape (June 2024): "I Call on Memory"

Beaver Magazine (May 2024): "On Visiting Puerto Rico for the First Time"

The Rumpus (April 2024): "In This Poem, My White, Jesus-Loving Dad with Glasses and Bad Jokes Is Not Dead"

Poetry Northwest (January 2024): "God Is Dog Spelled Backward"

underblong (August 2023): "Praying After Sex Is My Genre"

Four Way Review (November 2023): "Variations on a Theme by Ovid"

The Atlantic (January 2023): "The Bug"

The Recluse (2022): "Mom Belly Dances and Sees the Dead"

The Cincinnati Review (December 2020): "The Man I Do Not Sleep With"

A Long House (September 2020): "Cedar Waxwing"

A Long House (August 2020): "On Mercy"

The BreakBeat Poets Vol. 4: Latinext (April 2020): "¡Wepa!"

The Paris Review (The Daily, May 2020): "A Series of Small Miracles"

Slice (Fall 2019): "Grief Is a Thing That Wades"

Gratitude

Thank you to my press, Haymarket Books, for believing in my work and to Aricka Foreman, for soliciting my manuscript and making this book possible. Thank you to my editor, Maya Marshall, for helping me craft this book into a version of itself that I could not have imagined without her. To the readers of the earliest iterations of this manuscript— Hanif Abdurraqib, Dr. Joshua Bennett, and Rosebud Ben-Oni: I am grateful for their fervent belief in my vision.

I would not be the writer and person I am today without my mentors, Greg Pardlo and Vievee Francis. To Greg, who has believed in me from the start: this book is a result of his tutelage and care. To Vievee, who told me that "a part of the grace of God is the ability to wrestle with God": this book is my wrestling with the angel in the night. I thank them for making this version of myself possible.

To my family, friends, and colleagues, I am grateful for every phone call, writing session, word of kindness, and correction:

Sammy Adams, Malika Aisha, Jerriod Avant, Sasha Banks, Dante Clark, Hílda Davis, Trace DePass, Bee Ferguson, orion fleurs, Christopher Greggs, Luther Hughes, Tonya Ingram, Willie Kinard III, Nabila Lovelace, Ricky Maldonado, Rose Malenfant, Dr. Jonah Mixon-Webster, Airea D. Matthews, Nicholas Nichols, Nonso Njoku, Nkosi Nkululeko, Thiahera Nurse, Kwame Opoku-Duku, Gabriel Ramirez, Jayson P. Smith, Sahara Sidi, Sheena Som, Daniel Summerhill, Malcolm Tariq, Christa Watson, Mathew Watson, Tyriek White, Haolun Xu, and countless other beloveds.

A special thank you to Christopher Greggs who, in one of our countless conversations about poetry, said, "You know, Daniella, your poems are really about what we do with God," to which I interrupted, "Wait, can that please be the title of my book?" This collection would not be *What We Do with God* without him.

To my mother, Sadrie Toosie, who has encouraged me to follow my heart from the beginning and who gave me permission to write about her, "even if it doesn't put [her] in a good light": I'm indebted to her grace.

To my niece, Anani Acosta, and nephew, Christopher Acosta II, whom this all is meant to inspire: I thank them for being my inspiration to keep my dreams alive and live the "life . . . I would have chosen for myself from the beginning."

To my 2015 and 2016 Callaloo Creative Writing Workshop cohorts: I would not be the writer I am today without them.

To my MFA cohort and faculty at the University of Michigan Helen Zell Writers' Program, a special thanks to:

Akosua Zimba Afiriyie-Hwedie, 'Pemi Aguda, Mant Bares, Bryan Byrdlong, Franny Choi, Tarfia Faizullah, Augusta Funk, Linda Gregerson, Marlin Jenkins, A Van Jordan, Erika Nestor, and Monica Rico.

To my God, I'm grateful to live this life with you.

To Gabby: thank you for protecting us. You withstood through your silence. Now, we push back with a voice.

About the Author

Daniella Toosie-Watson (she/they) was shortlisted for the 2024 Oxford Poetry Prize and was a winner of the 2020 Discovery Contest. She has been published in *The Atlantic, The Paris Review, Oxford Poetry, Callaloo, Virginia Quarterly Review, Poet Lore*, and elsewhere. She received her MFA from the University of Michigan Helen Zell Writers' Program where she was awarded a Graduate Hopwood Award and Zell Fellowship. Daniella lives in New York.

About Haymarket Books

Haymarket Books is a radical, independent, nonprofit book publisher based in Chicago. Our mission is to publish books that contribute to struggles for social and economic justice. We strive to make our books a vibrant and organic part of social movements and the education and development of a critical, engaged, and internationalist Left.

We take inspiration and courage from our namesakes, the Haymarket Martyrs, who gave their lives fighting for a better world. Their 1886 struggle for the eight-hour day—which gave us May Day, the international workers' holiday—reminds workers around the world that ordinary people can organize and struggle for their own liberation. These struggles—against oppression, exploitation, environmental devastation, and war—continue today across the globe.

Since our founding in 2001, Haymarket has published more than nine hundred titles. Radically independent, we seek to drive a wedge into the risk-averse world of corporate book publishing. Our authors include Angela Y. Davis, Arundhati Roy, Keeanga-Yamahtta Taylor, Eve Ewing, Aja Monet, Mariame Kaba, Naomi Klein, Rebecca Solnit, Olúfẹmi O. Táíwò, Mohammed El Kurd, José Olivarez, Noam Chomsky, Winona LaDuke, Robyn Maynard, Leanne Betasamosake Simpson, Howard Zinn, Mike Davis, Marc Lamont Hill, Dave Zirin, Astra Taylor, and Amy Goodman, among many other leading writers of our time. We are also the trade publishers of the acclaimed Historical Materialism Book Series.

Haymarket also manages a vibrant community organizing and event space in Chicago, Haymarket House, the popular Haymarket Books Live event series and podcast, and the annual Socialism Conference.

Also Available from Haymarket Books

All the Blood Involved in Love, Maya Marshall

Ankle-Deep in Pacific Water, E. Hughes

Build Yourself a Boat, Camonghne Felix

Citizen Illegal, José Olivarez

Florida Water, aja monet

I Remember Death by Its Proximity to What I Love, Mahogany L. Browne

Like a Hammer: Poets on Mass Incarceration, edited by Diana Marie Delgado

A Map of My Want, Faylita Hicks

My Mother was a Freedom Fighter, aja monet

Nazar Boy, Tarik Dobbs

O Body, Dan "Sully" Sullivan

Rifqa, Mohammed El-Kurd

Super Sad Black Girl, Diamond Sharp

There Are Trans People Here, H. Melt

Too Much Midnight, Krista Franklin

We the Gathered Heat: Asian American and Pacific Islander Poetry, Performance, and Spoken Word, edited by Franny Choi, Bao Phi, Noʻu Revilla, and Terisa Siagatonu